A Month with
St Francis

Edited by Rima Devereaux

First published in Great Britain in 2018

Society for Promoting Christian Knowledge
36 Causton Street
London SW1P 4ST
www.spck.org.uk

British Library Cataloguing-in-Publication Data
A catalogue record for this book is available from the British Library

ISBN 978-0-281-07900-1
eBook ISBN 978-0-281-07901-8

Typeset by Fakenham Prepress Solutions, Fakenham, Norfolk NR21 8NN
Manufacture managed by Jellyfish
First printed in Great Britain by CPI
Subsequently digitally printed in Great Britain

eBook by Fakenham Prepress Solutions, Fakenham, Norfolk NR21 8NN

Produced on paper from sustainable forests

Introduction

St Francis of Assisi (1181–1216), the founder of the Franciscan Order, was the son of a wealthy cloth merchant. He rode off to fight in the Fourth Crusade but turned back when he had a dream in which God told him to return home. A defining moment in his conversion happened in the church of San Damiano in Assisi when he heard God say, 'Repair my church.' At first he took this literally as meaning the fabric of the building, but he came to understand it as wider, involving the corruption of the institutional Church. He and his companions went out to preach in rags, and he was known for his love of the natural world. He never became a priest, nor did he intend to found a religious order.

All of these extracts are taken from *The Little Flowers of Saint Francis*. This was a fourteenth-century collection of famous stories about Francis and his followers. These appealing and charming tales contain such episodes as his preaching to the birds, his taming of the wolf of Gubbio and his reception of the stigmata.

> In Francis's life there was both gaiety and austerity:
> You will not be able rationally to read the story of a man presented as a Mirror of Christ without understanding his final phase as a Man of Sorrows, and at least artistically appreciating the appropriateness of his receiving, in a cloud of mystery and isolation, inflicted by no human hand, the unhealed everlasting wounds that heal the world.[1]

Ultimately, there is a Francis that lies beyond all the stories: 'If you invited the real Francis to tea, he would likely insist on first standing out by the road to beg for his biscuits from passers-by, before joining you inside.'[2] The real Francis offers a fresh spirituality shot through with his characteristic sense of fellowship with nature.

A Month with
St Francis

DAY 1

Morning

It is first to be considered that the glorious St Francis, in all the acts of his life, was conformed to Christ the Blessed. And that even as Christ, at the beginning of his mission, chose twelve apostles who were to despise all worldly things and follow him in poverty and in the other virtues, so St Francis in the beginning chose for the foundation of his order twelve companions who were possessed of nothing but direst poverty . . . And even as those holy apostles were, above all, wondrous in their holiness and humility, and filled with the Holy Spirit, so those most holy companions of St Francis were men of . . . saintliness.

Evening

Now Bernard, when he beheld these most devout acts of St Francis . . . was moved and inspired by the Holy Spirit to change his manner of life . . . The priest . . . took the book and, having made the sign of the holy cross, opened it three times in the name of our Lord Jesus Christ . . . 'If you wish to be perfect, go and sell all that you have and give to the poor and follow me.' . . . Then St Francis said to Bernard, 'Behold the advice that Christ gives us. Go, therefore, do faithfully what you have heard, and blessed be the name of our Lord Jesus Christ, who has deigned to reveal to us the gospel life.'

DAY
2

Morning

St Francis said, 'Now tell me what you would have me do, for I have promised you holy obedience.' Then said Friar Bernard, 'I command you by holy obedience that every time we are together you rebuke and correct me harshly for all my faults.' Whereupon St Francis marvelled greatly, for Friar Bernard was of such exceeding sanctity that he held him in great reverence and in no wise worthy of reproof. From that moment, St Francis was careful to avoid being with Bernard much, because of the said obedience, in case it caused him to utter one word of reproof against him, for he knew him to be of such great holiness.

Evening

As they journeyed together, he found a poor sick man in a village by the way . . . St Francis and the other companions went their way to St James's. When they arrived there, they passed the night in prayer in the church of St James, where it was revealed to St Francis that he was to establish many friaries throughout the world, for his order was to spread and grow into a great multitude of friars. Whereupon, in accordance with this revelation, St Francis began to establish friaries in those lands. And as St Francis was returning by the way he came, he found Friar Bernard, and the sick man with whom he had left him healed perfectly.

DAY 3

Morning

Because St Francis and his companions were called and chosen by God to bear the cross of Christ in their hearts and in their works, and to preach it with their tongues, they seemed, and truly were, men crucified, in regard to their dress, the austerity of their lives, their acts and their deeds. Therefore they desired to endure shame and reproach for love of Christ rather than worldly honour or reverence or human praise. Indeed, they rejoiced in insults and were afflicted by honour; they went about the world as pilgrims and strangers, bearing nothing with them except Christ crucified.

Evening

St Francis . . . said to Friar Bernard, 'God the Father and our Lord Jesus Christ bless you with all spiritual and celestial blessings. You are the firstborn, chosen in this holy order to give evangelical example, and to follow Christ in gospel poverty, for not only did you give your own possessions and distribute them wholly and freely to the poor for love of Christ, but you offered also yourself to God in his order, a sacrifice of sweetness. You are blessed therefore by our Lord Jesus Christ and by me, poor little one, his servant, with blessings everlasting, walking and standing, watching and sleeping, living and dying.'

DAY
4

Morning

St Francis was once lodging on carnival day in the house of one of his devout followers on the shores of the lake of Perugia, and was inspired by God to go and pass that Lent on an island in the lake. Thus St Francis, on the night of Ash Wednesday, asked his disciple to carry him in his little boat to an island on which no one lived . . . St Francis took with him nothing except two small loaves . . . and so the friend departed and St Francis remained alone . . . And there he stayed for the whole of Lent, eating and drinking nothing but half of one of those small loaves.

Evening

Friar Leo asked [St Francis] . . . 'Father, please in God's name tell me where is perfect joy to be found?' And St Francis answered him like this: 'When we are come to St Mary of the Angels, wet through with rain, frozen with cold . . . and, when we knock at the door, the doorkeeper comes in a rage and says, "Who are you?" and we say, "We are two of your friars," and he answers, "You're not telling the truth; you are rather two knaves . . . begone!" and he doesn't open the door to us . . . then, if we endure patiently such cruelty . . . and believe humbly . . . that that doorkeeper truly knows us . . . O Friar Leo, write – there is perfect joy.'

DAY 5

Morning

Know that this I have from those eyes of the most high God, which everywhere see the righteous and the wicked, and because those most holy eyes have seen among sinners none more vile, more imperfect, nor a greater sinner than I, therefore since he has found no viler creature on earth to accomplish the marvellous work he intends, he has chosen me to confound the nobility, the majesty, the might, the beauty and the wisdom of the world; in order to make manifest that every virtue and every good thing comes from him the Creator, and not from the creature.

Evening

'O Friar Masseo . . . I desire that you take upon yourself the offices of doorkeeper, of almoner and of cook, in order that your companions may give themselves up to contemplation; and when the other friars are eating, you will eat outside the door of the friary so that you can satisfy with some sweet words of God those who come to the convent when they knock, and so that no friar other than you needs to go outside. Do this through the merit of holy obedience.' Then Friar Masseo drew back his cowl and inclined his head and humbly received and fulfilled this command.

DAY

6

Morning

And as St Francis remained in prayer a long while, with many tears and great devotion, the holy Apostles Peter and Paul appeared to him in great splendour, and said, 'Because you ask and desire to serve that which Christ and his holy Apostles served, our Lord Jesus Christ sent us to you to announce that your prayer is heard, and that God grants you and your followers the perfect treasure of holiest poverty. And from him also we say to thee, that whoever, following your example, shall pursue this desire perfectly, he is assured of the blessedness of life eternal; and you and all your followers shall be blessed by God.'

Evening

St Francis . . . entered into the field and began to preach to the birds that were on the ground . . . And the substance of the sermon St Francis preached was this: 'My little sisters the birds, much are you beholden to God your Creator, and always and in every place you ought to praise him . . . Again, you are beholden to him for the element of air which he has appointed for you; moreover, you do not sow, neither do you reap, and God feeds you and gives you the rivers and the fountains for your drink.' . . . Finally, his sermon ended, St Francis made the sign of the holy cross over them and gave them leave to depart.

DAY

7

Morning

St Francis, holy father of all and general minister, expounded the word of God with a fervent spirit and preached to them in a loud voice whatever the Holy Spirit put into his mouth. And for the text of his sermon he took these words: 'My children, great things have we promised to God; things exceedingly great has God promised to us, if we observe those we have promised to him; and certainly do we await those things promised to us. Brief is the joy of this world; the pain that comes hereafter is everlasting. Small is the pain of this life, but the glory of the life to come is infinite.'

Evening

'These fair garments of fine cloth we wear are given to us by God in lieu of the coarse tunics we wore in the order; and the glorious brightness that you behold is given to us by God for the humility and patience, and for the holy poverty and obedience and chastity we kept even to the last. Therefore, my son, do not let it be hard for you to wear the sackcloth of the order, which is so fruitful, because if, clothed in the sackcloth of St Francis, for love of Christ you despise the world and mortify your flesh and valiantly fight against the devil, you, with us, shall have a like raiment and great brightness of glory.'

DAY

8

Morning

In the days when St Francis lived in the city of Gubbio, a huge wolf, terrible and fierce, appeared in the neighbourhood . . . Then St Francis spoke to him thus: 'Friar wolf, you have worked much evil in these parts, and have wrought grievous ill, destroying and slaying God's creatures without his leave . . . But, friar wolf, I would willingly make peace with them and with you, so that you injure them no more.' . . . Now when St Francis had spoken these words, the wolf, moving his body and his tail and his ears, and bowing his head, made signs that he accepted what had been said, and would abide thereby.

Evening

A certain youth one day, having snared many turtle doves, was taking them to market when St Francis met him. And St Francis, who always had singular compassion for gentle creatures, gazed upon those doves with a pitying eye, and said to the youth, 'O good youth, please give them to me, lest birds so gentle that chaste, humble and faithful souls are compared to them in the Scriptures fall into the hands of cruel men who would kill them.' Straightaway the youth, inspired by God, gave them all to St Francis, who received them into his bosom and began to speak sweetly to them: 'O my little sisters, you simple doves, innocent and chaste, how did you suffer yourselves to be caught? Now will I rescue you from death.'

DAY

9

Morning

By miracle divine, wherever St Francis touched him with his holy hands, the leprosy departed and the flesh became perfectly whole. And even as the flesh began to heal, the soul began to heal also; whereupon the leper, seeing the leprosy on the way to leaving him, began to have great compunction and repentance for his sins, and bitterly he began to weep; so that while the body was outwardly cleansed of the leprosy by the washing with water, the soul within was cleansed of sin by amendment and tears. And being wholly healed, as much in body as in soul, he humbly confessed his sins.

Evening

Now in those days three famous robbers, who infested the country and wrought much evil there, came to the said friary and besought the said warden, Friar Angel, to give them food to eat. And the warden answered them, rebuking them harshly . . . at which they, perturbed, departed in great fury. And lo, St Francis appeared outside the friary . . . And when the warden related to him how he had driven the robbers away, St Francis chided him severely, saying he had behaved cruelly, since sinners were better drawn to God by gentleness than by cruel reproof.

DAY

10

Morning

And so wondrously he preached that he seemed to speak with the voice of an angel rather than of a man; his celestial words seemed to pierce the hearts of those that heard them, even as sharp arrows, so that during his sermon a great multitude of men and women were converted to repentance. Among whom were two students of noble birth from the Marches of Ancona, one named Pellegrino, the other Rinieri: and being touched in their hearts by divine inspiration through the said sermon, they came to St Francis saying they desired wholly to forsake the world and be numbered among his friars.

Evening

Even as our Lord Jesus Christ said in the gospel, 'I know my sheep, and my own know me' . . . so the blessed father St Francis, like a good shepherd, knew all the merits and the virtues of his companions by divine revelation, and likewise their failings. By this means he knew how to provide the best remedy for each, that is to say, by humbling the proud, exalting the humble, reproving vice and praising virtue . . . How St Francis knew the failings of his friars is clearly manifest in Friar Elias, whom many times he chided for his pride; and in Friar John della Cappella, to whom he foretold that he was to hang himself by the neck.

DAY

11

Morning

St Clare had the table laid and set loaves of bread on it so that the holy father might bless them . . . The holy father answers, 'Sister Clare, most faithful one, I desire that you bless this bread, and make over it the sign of the most holy cross of Christ, to which you have wholly devoted yourself.' . . . Then St Clare, as a true daughter of obedience, devoutly blessed the bread with the sign of the most holy cross. Marvellous to tell, immediately the sign of the cross appeared on all those loaves, represented most beautifully.

Evening

Friar Giles answered . . . 'No sooner had we embraced together, than the light of wisdom revealed and manifested his heart to me and mine to him, and thus, by divine power, as we looked in each other's breasts, we knew better what I would say to him and he to me than if we had spoken with our mouths; and greater consolation had we than if we had sought to explain with our lips what we felt in our hearts. For, because of the defect of human speech, which cannot express clearly the mysteries and secrets of God, words would have left us disconsolate rather than consoled.'

DAY

12

Morning

Once, when St Clare was so grievously sick that she could in no way go to say the office in church with the other nuns, and seeing that when the feast of the Nativity of Christ came all the others went to matins, while she remained in bed, she grew ill at ease that she could not go with them and enjoy that spiritual consolation. But Jesus Christ, her spouse, not willing to leave her thus disconsolate, caused her to be miraculously borne to the church of St Francis and to be present at the whole office of matins, and at the midnight Mass; and moreover, she received the holy communion, and then was borne back to her bed.

Evening

And as soon as the previously mentioned Friar Leo had told his vision in due order, St Francis said, 'What you have seen is true. The mighty stream is this world; the friars that were drowned therein are they that followed not the teachings of the gospel, and especially in regard to most high poverty. But they that passed over without peril are those friars that seek after no earthly or carnal thing, nor possess anything in this world; but, temperate in food and clothing, are glad, following Christ naked on the cross, and bear joyously and willingly the burden and sweet yoke of Christ and of most holy obedience. Therefore they pass with ease from this temporal life to life eternal.'

DAY

13

Morning

That wonderful vessel of the Holy Spirit, St Anthony of Padua, one of the chosen disciples and companions of St Francis, he that St Francis called his vicar, was once preaching in the consistory before the pope and the cardinals, in which consistory were men of diverse nations – French, Germans, Slavonians and English – and diverse other tongues throughout the world. Inflamed by the Holy Spirit, he expounded the word of God so effectually, so devoutly, so subtly, so sweetly, so clearly and so wisely that they that were in the consistory, albeit from different nations, clearly understood all his words distinctly, even as though he had spoken to each one of them in his native tongue.

Evening

There came towards the bank such a multitude of fishes, great and small and middling . . . and all held their heads out of the water in great peace and gentleness and perfect order, and remained intent on the lips of St Anthony . . . St Anthony began to preach to them solemnly, and spoke thus: 'You fishes, my brothers, much are you bound, according to your power, to thank God our Creator, who has given you so noble an element for your habitation; for at your pleasure have you waters, sweet and salt, and he has given you many places of refuge to shelter you from the tempests; he has likewise given you a pure and clear element, and food whereby you can live.'

DAY

14

Morning

In the early days of the Order of St Francis, and while the saint was still alive, a youth of Assisi came to the order, who was called Friar Simon, whom God adorned and endowed with such grace and such contemplation and elevation of mind that all his life he was a mirror of holiness, even as described by those who were with him a long time. Very seldom was he seen outside his cell, and if at any time he was seen with the friars, he was always speaking of God. He had never been through the schools, yet so profoundly and so loftily did he speak of God, and of the love of Christ, that his words seemed supernatural.

Evening

The friars prayed [Friar Conrad] for love of God and of his charity to admonish a young friar that was in the settlement, who bore himself so childishly, so disorderly and dissolutely, that he disturbed both old and young of that community during the divine offices, and cared little or naught for the observances of the Rule. Whereupon Friar Conrad, in compassion for that youth, and at the prayers of the friars, called the said youth apart one day, and in fervour of charity spake to him words of admonition, so effectual and so divine, that by the operation of divine grace he straightway became changed from a child to an old man in manners.

DAY

15

Morning

Now this friar loved solitude and seldom spoke; yet, when anything was asked of him, he answered so graciously and so wisely that he seemed an angel rather than a man; and he excelled in prayer and in contemplation, and the friars held him in great reverence. The friar, having run the course of his virtuous life, according to divine disposition, fell sick to the point of death, so that he could eat nothing; and, in addition, he would receive no medicine for his body, but all his trust was in the heavenly physician, Jesus Christ the blessed, and in his blessed Mother, by whom, through divine clemency, he was held worthy to be mercifully visited and healed.

Evening

[Friar James of La Massa] beheld Christ seated on an exceedingly great, pure white throne, to which Christ called St Francis and gave him a cup, full of the spirit of life, and sent him forth, saying, 'Go and visit your friars and give them a drink from this cup of the spirit of life; for the spirit of Satan will rise up against them and will smite them, and many of them will fall and not rise again.' And Christ gave two angels to St Francis to accompany him. And then St Francis came and held forth the cup of life to his friars . . . They that took it devoutly and drank it all became immediately bright and shining as the sun.

DAY

16

Morning

But since God has singular care of his children, and gives them things according to different seasons, now consolation, now tribulation, now prosperity, now adversity, just as he sees their need, either to strengthen them in humility or to kindle within them greater desire for celestial things; now it pleased divine goodness to withdraw, after three years, from the said Friar John this ray and this flame of divine love, and to deprive him of all spiritual consolation. As a result, Friar John remained bereft of the light and the love of God, and totally disconsolate and afflicted and sorrowing.

Evening

And Friar John, beholding him and knowing full well that it was the Christ, immediately flung himself at his feet, and with piteous tears entreated him most humbly and said, 'Help me, my Lord, for without you, O my sweetest Saviour, I wander in darkness and in tears; without you, most gentle Lamb, I dwell in anguish and in torment and in fear; without you, I am stripped of all good, and blind, for you are Christ Jesus, true light of souls; without you I am lost and damned, for you are the Life of souls and Life of life; without you I am barren and withered, for you are the fountain of every good gift and of every grace.'

DAY

17

Morning

And in the pathway of the wood, on which the blessed
feet of Christ had trod, and for a good space round about,
Friar John perceived that same fragrance and beheld
that splendour for a long time afterwards, whenever
he went there. And Friar John, coming to himself after
that rapture and after the bodily presence of Christ had
vanished, remained so illumined in his soul and in the
abyss of the divine nature that, even though he was not a
learned man by reason of human study, nevertheless he
understood wondrously and explained the most subtle
and lofty questions touching the divine Trinity and the
profound mysteries of the holy Scriptures.

Evening

[Friar John] departed from that place and went to visit the said Friar James at Moliano, and, finding the sickness so heavily upon him that he could hardly speak, he announced to him the death of the body and the salvation and glory of his soul . . . At this, Friar James rejoiced gladly in spirit and in countenance . . . and with cheerful appearance gave thanks to him for the good tidings he had brought, commending himself devoutly to him . . . The hour of his passing away drew near, and Friar James began to recite devoutly that verse from the Psalms: *In pace in idipsum dormiam et requiescam*, which is to say, 'I will both lay me down in peace and sleep.' This verse said, he passed from this life with glad and joyful countenance.

DAY
18

Morning

And then he perceived clearly how every created thing was related to its Creator, and how God is above, is within, is without, is beside all created things. Thereafter he perceived one God in three Persons, and three Persons in one God, and the infinite love that made the Son of God become flesh in obedience to the Father. And finally he perceived, in that vision, how that no other way was there whereby the soul might ascend to God and have eternal life except through the blessed Christ, who is the Way, the Truth and the Life of the soul.

Evening

And while [Friar John] was meditating on the words of the consecration of the body of Christ . . . while he was considering the infinite love of Christ, and that he had been willing to redeem us not only with his precious blood but likewise to leave us his most worthy body and blood as food for our souls, the love of sweet Jesus began so to wax within him, and with such great fervour and tenderness, that his soul could no longer endure such sweetness. And he cried out with a loud voice, as one drunk in spirit, endlessly repeating to himself, *Hoc est corpus meum*: for as he spoke these words . . . he was illumined by the Holy Spirit in all the deep and lofty mysteries of that most high sacrament.

DAY

19

Morning

And at last this Roland said to St Francis, 'I have a mountain in Tuscany, called the mount of La Verna, that would be most suitable for devout contemplation; it is very solitary and just right for those who desire to do penance in a place far away from the world, or to lead a solitary life. And if it so please you, I would like to give it to you and your companions for the salvation of my soul.' St Francis, hearing this generous offer of a thing he so much desired, rejoiced with exceedingly great joy, and praising and giving thanks, first to God and then to Roland, spoke to him thus: 'Roland . . . I will send some of my companions to you, and you will show them this mountain.'

Evening

And at last, finding [Christ] in the secret places of his soul, now [St Francis] spoke with him reverently as his Lord; now he gave answer to him as his judge; again he besought him as a father, and yet again he reasoned with him as a friend. On that night, and in that wood, his companions, after they awoke, stood listening and wondering what he was doing, and they saw and heard him with tears and cries devoutly entreat God's mercy for sinners. Then he was heard and seen to bewail, with a loud voice, the Passion of Christ, even as if he saw it with his own eyes. And in that same night they saw him praying with his arms held in the form of a cross.

DAY

20

Morning

Then St Francis made his companions sit down, and instructed them, and whoever would desire to live like religious, in hermitages, about the manner of the life that they should lead. And, among other things, he laid upon them the single-minded observance of holy poverty . . . 'God has called us to this holy rule of life for the salvation of the world, and has made this covenant between us and the world, that we offer a good example to the world . . . Let us persevere, then, in holy poverty, because that is the way of perfection, and the sign and pledge of everlasting riches.'

Evening

A few days later, as St Francis was standing beside the said cell, considering the form of the mountain, and marvelling at the huge clefts and caverns in the mighty rocks, he took himself off to pray; and then it was revealed to him by God that these clefts, which are so marvellous, had been miraculously made at the hour of the Passion of Christ, when, according to the gospel, the rocks were rent asunder. And this, God willed, should manifestly appear on the mount of La Verna, because there the Passion of our Lord Jesus Christ was to be renewed, through love and pity, in the soul of St Francis, and in his body by the imprinting of the sacred, hallowed stigmata.

DAY

21

Morning

As St Francis one day was meditating on his death, and on the state of his order after his death, and saying, 'Lord God, what will become of your poor little household that of your goodness you have committed to me, a sinner? Who shall comfort them? Who shall correct them? Who shall pray to you for them?' And while he was uttering such words, the angel sent by God appeared to him, and comforted him with these words: 'I tell you, in God's name, that the profession of your order shall not fail until the Judgement Day, and none shall be so great a sinner, but that if he loves your order in his heart, he shall find mercy in God's sight.'

Evening

Then God said, 'Search your heart and offer me what you find there.' I searched there and found a ball of gold, and this I offered to God; and I did this three times, just as God had asked me three times. And then three times I knelt down, and blessed and gave thanks to God that he had given me what I needed to offer to him. And immediately it was given to me to know that those three offers signified holy obedience, most exalted poverty and most resplendent chastity, which God disclosed to me by his grace, to observe so perfectly that my conscience accused me of nothing.

DAY

22

Morning

This wonderful vision having vanished, after a significant time, this secret converse left in the heart of St Francis a burning flame of divine love, exceedingly great, and in his flesh a marvellous image and imprint of the Passion of Christ. For the marks of the nails soon began to be seen on the hands and feet of St Francis, in the same manner as he had then seen them in the body of Jesus Christ crucified that had appeared to him in the form of a seraph. And thus his hands and feet seemed nailed through the middle with nails, the heads of which were in the palms of his hands and in the soles of his feet, outside the flesh.

Evening

And although those most holy wounds, in so far as they were imprinted by Christ, gave him great joy in his heart, nevertheless to his flesh and to his bodily senses they gave unbearable pain. For that reason, being constrained by necessity, he chose Friar Leo, simplest and purest among the friars, to reveal all these things to. And he let him see and touch those holy wounds and bind them with bandages to ease the pain and staunch the blood that issued and ran from them; at the time of his sickness, he allowed the dressings to be changed often, even every day, except from Thursday evening to Saturday morning.

DAY

23

Morning

[The belly of the young child brought to Francis] was so swollen and so deformed that when he stood up he could not see his feet; and placing this child before him, [his mother] besought St Francis to pray to God for him. And St Francis first betook himself to prayer, and then, the prayer ended, laid his holy hands on the child's belly, and immediately all the swelling was down and he was wholly healed; and St Francis gave him back to his mother, who received him with the greatest joy and led him home, giving thanks to God and to St Francis. And she willingly showed her son healed to all those from around the countryside who came to her house to see him.

Evening

[Friar Leo] beheld a cross, which was exceedingly beautiful, on which was the figure of the Crucified, going before St Francis, who was riding in front of him; and so closely did that cross conform to the movements of St Francis, that when he stopped, it stopped; and when he went on, it went on: and that cross shone with such great brightness that not only did the face of St Francis shine resplendent, but likewise the whole area around him was illumined. And that brightness endured even up to the time that St Francis entered the friary of St Mary of the Angels.

DAY

24

Morning

There was the Lady Jacqueline, the noblest lady of Rome, with her two sons, who were Roman senators, and with a great company of horsemen, and they entered in; and the Lady Jacqueline goes straight to the infirmary and comes to St Francis. And at her coming St Francis felt great joy and consolation, and she likewise, when she saw him in the flesh and was able to speak with him . . . And when he had eaten, and was much comforted, the Lady Jacqueline knelt at the feet of St Francis and took those most holy feet, marked and adorned with the wounds of Christ, and kissed them, and bathed his feet with her tears, and did this with such exceedingly great devotion that the friars who stood around seemed to see the Magdalen herself at the feet of Jesus Christ.

Evening

Setting aside all the miracles of the sacred and holy stigmata of St Francis, which may be read in his legend, let the following be known, in conclusion of this consideration: St Francis appeared one night to Pope Gregory IX, as he afterwards related, when he was in some doubt about the wound in the side of St Francis, and lifting up his right arm a little, the saint revealed the wound in his side, and asked for a flask, and had it brought to him. And St Francis had it held under the wound in his side, and indeed it seemed to the Pope that he saw the flask filled to the brim with blood mingled with water, which issued from the wound; and from that moment all doubt departed from him.

DAY

25

Morning

That the devil was unable to endure the purity of Friar Juniper's innocence and his deep humility is shown in this story. Once upon a time, a man possessed with a devil fled from his home in an unaccustomed manner and with much rage for seven miles along obscure paths. And when he was overtaken by his kinsfolk who followed after him with bitter grief, they asked why in his flight he had taken such devious paths. He answered, 'The reason is this: because that fool Juniper was coming this way, and I could neither endure his presence nor bear to encounter him, I fled through these woods.'

Evening

So much pity and compassion had Friar Juniper for the poor that when he saw anyone ill clad or naked, he would shortly take off his tunic and the cowl from his cloak, and give them to poor souls such as these. Therefore the warden commanded him, by obedience, not to give away the whole of his tunic, nor any part of his habit. Now it so happened that Friar Juniper, after a few days had passed, came across a poor creature, well-nigh naked, who asked alms of him for love of God, to whom he said with great compassion, 'I haven't got anything except my tunic to give you . . . but if you take it off my back, I will not stop you.'

DAY

26

Morning

Once upon a time, Friar Juniper made a vow in this manner to keep silence for six months. The first day, for love of the heavenly Father. The second day, for love of his Son, Jesus Christ. The third day, for love of the Holy Ghost. The fourth day, for reverence of the most holy Virgin Mary; and so in this order, every day, for six months, he observed silence for love of some saint . . . One time, Friar Juniper, desiring truly to abase himself, stripped himself down to his undergarments; and having made a bundle of his habit, he placed his clothes on his head and, entering Viterbo, went to the marketplace to be mocked.

Evening

Once, Friar Juniper was left alone in a small friary because all the friars . . . had to go out from the friary. The warden said to him, 'Friar Juniper, we all have to go out; make sure, therefore, that when we return you have some food ready cooked for the refreshment of the friars.' Friar Juniper replied, 'Of course, willingly, leave it to me!' And all the friars having gone out . . . Friar Juniper said, 'What unprofitable care is this, for one friar to be lost in the kitchen and far away from all prayer! Truly, if I am left here to cook, this time I will cook so much that all the friars, and even more, shall have enough to eat for a fortnight.'

DAY

27

Morning

Now, as it pleased God, this Friar Amazialbene died with the highest reputation; and Friar Juniper, hearing of his death, felt a greater sadness of spirit than he had ever felt in his life for the loss of any material thing. And he expressed outwardly the great bitterness that was within him, and said, 'Woe is me! . . . now no good thing is left to me, and all the world is out of joint . . . Were it not that I should have no peace from the other friars, I would go to his grave and take away his head, and with the skull I would make me two bowls: from one I would always eat in devout memory of him; and from the other I would drink whenever I was thirsty or wanted a drink.'

Evening

[Friar Giles] fell on his knees on the ground before St Francis, and humbly asked him to receive him into his company, for love of God. St Francis, gazing on the devout appearance of Friar Giles, answered and said, 'Dearest brother, God has conferred on you a very great grace. If the emperor came to Assisi, and wanted to make one of the men of this city his knight . . . ought he not to rejoice greatly? How much greater joy should you receive in that God hath chosen you for his knight and most beloved servant, to observe the perfect way of the holy gospel? Therefore, be steadfast and constant in the vocation to which God has called you.'

DAY

28

Morning

Friar Giles went, with the permission of St Francis, to visit the Holy Sepulchre of Christ, and came to the port of Brindisi, where he stayed for many days, for there was no ship ready. And Friar Giles, desiring to live by his labour, begged a pitcher and, filling it with water, went about the city crying, 'Who lacks water?' And for his toil he received bread and things necessary for the life of the body, both for himself and for his companion. And then he crossed the seas, and visited with great devotion the Holy Sepulchre of Christ and the other holy places.

Evening

Friar Giles answered, 'My son, have you not yet learned or known what prayer is? True prayer is to do the will of our superior; and it is an indication of great pride in him who, having put his neck under the yoke of holy obedience, refuses it for any reason, in order to follow his own will, even though it may seem to him that he is doing a work of greater perfection. The perfectly obedient religious is like a knight mounted on a mighty steed, by whose power he passes fearlessly through the midst of the fray; and, to the contrary, the disobedient and complaining and unwilling religious is like one who is mounted on a lean and infirm and vicious horse.'

DAY 29

Morning

When Friar Giles was once living in the friary at Rome, he was minded to live by manual labour, as he had always done since he entered the Order, and he spent his day in the following way. Early in the morning, he heard Mass with much devotion, then he went to the wood that was eight miles outside Rome and carried a faggot of wood back on his shoulders, and sold it for bread, or anything at all to eat . . . Seldom did Friar Giles work the whole day through, for he always bargained to have some period of time to say the canonical hours and not fail in his mental prayers.

Evening

All things whatsoever that can be thought in the heart or told with the tongue, or seen with the eyes, or touched with the hands – all are as nothing in respect of, and compared with, those things that cannot be thought or seen or touched. All the saints and all the sages who have passed away, and all those who are in this present life, and all who shall come after us – who spoke or wrote, or who shall speak or write of God – have not and will not be able to show forth as much of God as a grain of millet would be in respect of, or in comparison with, the heavens and the earth; no, a thousand thousand times less.

DAY

30

Morning

He that with steadfast humility and patience suffers and endures tribulation, through fervent love of God, soon shall attain to great grace and virtues, and shall be lord of this world, and shall have a foretaste of the next and glorious world. Everything that a man does, good or evil, he does it to himself; therefore, be not offended with him who harms you, rather show him humble patience, and only grieve within for his sin, having compassion on him and praying to God earnestly for him.

Evening

The slothful man loses both this world and the next; he bears no fruit for himself and does not profit another. It is impossible for a person to gain virtue without diligence and hard work. When you can dwell in a safe place, don't stand in a perilous place: the one who abides in a safe place is the one who strives and suffers and works and toils through God, and for the Lord God; and not through fear of punishment, or for a price, but for love of God. The one who refuses to suffer and labour for love of Christ, truly that person refuses the glory of Christ; and just as diligence is useful and profitable to us, so is negligence always against us.

DAY 31

Morning

Many sorrows and many woes will the miserable man suffer who puts his desire and his heart and his hope in earthly things, whereby he forsakes and loses heavenly things, and in the end will even lose also these earthly things. The eagle soars very high, but if she had tied a weight to her wings she would not be able to fly very high: and so too with the weight of earthly things, a man cannot fly high, indeed he cannot attain to perfection. But the wise man who binds the weight of the remembrance of death and judgement to the wings of his heart could not, for the great fear of those things, go astray nor chase the vanities and false riches of this world.

Evening

What does it profit a man to fast much and pray and give alms and afflict himself with the overpowering sense of heavenly things if he fails to reach the blessed haven of the salvation he desires, that is, the haven of good and steadfast perseverance? Sometimes this occurs: a certain ship, beautiful and mighty and strong and new, and filled with great riches, is seen on the seas; and it happens that, through some storm, or through the fault of the helmsman, the ship perishes and is wrecked; the ship tragically sinks and fails to arrive at the desired haven.

Notes and source

Notes

1   G. K. Chesterton, *St. Francis of Assisi* (New York: Dover
    Publications, n. d.), p. 6.
2   Jon M. Sweeney, *When Saint Francis Saved the Church:
    How a Converted Medieval Troubadour Created a
    Spiritual Vision for the Ages* (Notre Dame, IN: Ave Maria
    Press, 2015).

Source

The Little Flowers of Saint Francis, translated by Thomas
Okey (Mineola, NY: Dover Publications, 2003), reprint of *The
Little Flowers of St. Francis* (New York: E. P. Dutton & Co.,
1963). The text has been lightly modernized by Hannah Ward
and Jennifer Wild.

The Little Flowers of Saint Francis

Day 1: Morning, ch. 1, p. 1; Evening, ch. 2, pp. 3–4
Day 2: Morning, ch. 3, p. 6; Evening, ch. 4, pp. 6–7
Day 3: Morning, ch. 5, p. 9; Evening, ch. 6, p. 11
Day 4: Morning, ch. 7, pp. 12–13; Evening, ch. 8, p. 14
Day 5: Morning, ch. 10, p. 17; Evening, ch. 12, p. 19
Day 6: Morning, ch. 13, p. 22; Evening, ch. 16, pp. 26–7
Day 7: Morning, ch. 18, p. 29; Evening, ch. 20, p. 34
Day 8: Morning, ch. 21, pp. 34–5; Evening, ch. 22, p. 37
Day 9: Morning, ch. 25, p. 41; Evening, ch. 26, p. 42
Day 10: Morning, ch. 27, p. 47; Evening, ch. 31, pp. 53–4
Day 11: Morning, ch. 33, pp. 55–6; Evening, ch. 34, p. 57
Day 12: Morning, ch. 35, p. 57; Evening, ch. 36, p. 58
Day 13: Morning, ch. 39, p. 62; Evening, ch. 40, p. 63
Day 14: Morning, ch. 41, p. 64; Evening, ch. 43, p. 68
Day 15: Morning, ch. 47, p. 75; Evening, ch. 48, p. 77
Day 16: Morning, ch. 49, p. 79; Evening, ch. 49, p. 80
Day 17: Morning, ch. 49, pp. 81–2; Evening, ch. 51, p. 83
Day 18: Morning, ch. 52, p. 85; Evening, ch. 53, p. 85

'Touching the Sacred and Holy Stigmas'
Day 19: Morning, p. 89; Evening, p. 91
Day 20: Morning, p. 93; Evening, p. 94
Day 21: Morning, p. 95; Evening, p. 100
Day 22: Morning, p. 102; Evening, p. 103
Day 23: Morning, p. 105; Evening, p. 107
Day 24: Morning, p. 111; Evening, p. 119

'The Life of Friar Juniper'
Day 25: Morning, pp. 121–2; Evening, p. 124
Day 26: Morning, pp. 126–7; Evening, p. 128
Day 27: Morning, p. 130; Evening, p. 132

'The Life of the Blessed Friar Giles'
Day 28: Morning, p. 133; Evening, p. 134
Day 29: Morning, pp. 134–5

'Certain Doctrines and Notable Sayings of Friar Giles'
Day 29: Evening, p. 139
Day 30: Morning, p. 142; Evening, pp. 144–5
Day 31: Morning, p. 147; Evening, p. 157